Advance praise for:
Build Your Castles in the Air:
Thoreau's Inspiring Advice
for Success
in Business (and Life)
in the 21st Century

"*I love Thoreau and I especially love this inspirational treatment of his work.*"

—Dr. Wayne Dyer
NY Times #1 bestselling author; self-empowerment leader

"*In Congress, in business, and as a mother of two children, I've seen first-hand the demands that our fast-forward, high-pressure culture puts on individuals, on families and on organizations. Through Build Your Castles in the Air, Thoreau's timeless wisdom and Chuck Hansen's modern insights offer simple yet intelligent solutions to the professional and personal dilemmas we all face, every day. Read this book and bring balance and genuine success—the type that truly matters—into your life.*"

—Honorable Susan Molinari
Former member of Congress;
president and CEO of The Washington Group

"*This book embraces the human side of our rapidly and substantially changing world and will be of great benefit to both individuals and organizations. As someone who has been active in leadership development for three decades, I believe Build Your Castles in the Air is a rich reflection and dialogue vehicle for enhancing a sense of purpose, strategy, mission or corporate responsibility.*"

—Victoria Guthrie
Senior fellow, Innovative Program Initiatives
Center for Creative Leadership

"*I thoroughly enjoyed Build Your Castles in the Air by Chuck Hansen. After finishing this thoughtful book I felt like it really contained two books in one. First, the author helps interpret the wise but sometimes complex writings of Thoreau in a clear manner with surprising relevance to today's business and personal life. However, it was Hansen's own commentary and thoughts that I found most valuable. I found myself wishing for more of the author's observations and suggestions for current day business issues. With every turn of the page I found comments that offered specific advice that I or others I know are facing today. I also felt that the book, and wisdom by both Thoreau and Hansen, was uplifting and offered easy-to-grasp ideas on how to survive and thrive in today's business world.*"

—Craig Shanklin
Former chief operating officer, Correlogic Systems

"Hansen's book puts a context around a great work and allows the reader to sample and deeply consider the magnificent work of Henry David Thoreau by topic. I especially liked the personal commentary and the selections from Civil Disobedience. Hansen's comments bring focus and relevance to Thoreau's work."

—Louis Castle
Vice president, Electronic Arts;
former GM and co-founder of Westwood Studios

Build Your Castles in the Air

Build Your Castles in the Air

◆

Thoreau's Inspiring Advice for Success in Business (and Life) in the 21st Century

Chuck Hansen

iUniverse, Inc.
New York Lincoln Shanghai

Build Your Castles in the Air
Thoreau's Inspiring Advice for Success in Business (and Life) in the 21st Century

Copyright © 2005 by Charles D. Hansen, III

iUniverse books may be ordered through booksellers or by contacting:

iUniverse
2021 Pine Lake Road, Suite 100
Lincoln, NE 68512
www.iuniverse.com
1-800-Authors (1-800-288-4677)

ISBN-13: 978-0-595-37251-5 (pbk)
ISBN-13: 978-0-595-81648-4 (ebk)
ISBN-10: 0-595-37251-1 (pbk)
ISBN-10: 0-595-81648-7 (ebk)

Printed in the United States of America

His robust common sense, armed with stout hands, keen perceptions and strong will, cannot yet account for the superiority which shone in his simple and hidden life. I must add the cardinal fact, that there was an excellent wisdom in him, proper to a rare class of men, which showed him the material world as a means and a symbol.

—"Thoreau"
Ralph Waldo Emerson

Contents

Introduction

During my career in politics, government and with three Fortune 500 companies, I have come to realize that much of the productivity and economic gains of recent years have been achieved by asking workers to do more with less, and in less time. Personal time, peace of mind and balance have been squeezed out of people's lives by the unrelenting pursuit of greater productivity and quarter-over-quarter profit increases. And technology, rather than assisting workers, has in fact served only to speed up the treadmill on which we all are running.

Upon reaching this conclusion, I realized that the familiar echo I could hear in this concept was the crystal-clear thinking of Henry David Thoreau. Picking up *Walden*, I almost immediately turned to his scathing indictment of the technological miracle of his day: "We do not ride on the railroad; it rides upon us." These words captured perfectly my thoughts about the effect of modern technology on today's worker.

As I continued through *Walden*, I was shocked by how much of that classic work applies to today's corporate world! Thoreau brings a stunning clarity of thought and insight into the increasingly grinding 21st Century work experience—not only for the worker bees, who are most often at the receiving end of corporate "stretch goals," but for their managers, most of whom are trying to find a humane way to manage their employees while simultaneously carrying out the often-inhuman demands of the organization.

In *Walden*, Thoreau brilliantly displays the "excellent wisdom," described by his friend Ralph Waldo Emerson, which allowed him to view the world not only as an environment worthy of reverence and respect, but as a source of penetrating lessons for leading a worthwhile life.

Reading Thoreau's masterpiece, it occurred to me that a collection of these gems would bring some desperately needed perspective to the increasingly harsh 21st Century work environment. Knowing that the resource most lacking in most people's lives is time, I determined that the best approach would be to excerpt from *Walden* the snippets of wisdom that applied to the most common problems faced by employees and managers in corporate America. I've also included a few quotes from Thoreau's classic anti-government essay "Civil Disobedience" (marked by a "CD").

I have arranged the quotes from *Walden* by current-day issues to which they apply, and I have added commentary—reflections from personal experience, as well as contributions from some of history's greatest thinkers, from Jesus Christ to Abraham Maslow.

Then, in the interest of accessibility, I organized the quotes around seven subject areas. I lead off with Finding Your Calling, because the first order of business should always be to get in tune with your higher purpose. However, if you are in the middle of a work-day emergency, feel free to skip ahead in the book to Managing Your Day-to-Day Work, which is intended to provide the reader with triage techniques for typical workday problems.

Following that, I shift to the longer-term and deeper issue of Managing Your Career, because I believe that long-term happiness with work requires a long-term perspective on work. Then I return to the more immediate issues of Managing the Business; Managing Your People; Managing Your Working Relationships; and, Managing the Business Environment.

Despite all of this segmenting and separating, though, one of the first things you will learn from Thoreau is that all elements of life (indeed, of all creation) are interconnected. So, to the extent that you manage your life well, you also manage your day-to-day work well, and *visa-versa*.

The goal of this book is to make Thoreau's wisdom more accessible, in bite-sized pieces to chew on during five-minute "lunch hours," and thereby help bring to harried readers the peace of mind and purpose that Thoreau's work has brought for me.

One additional, personal note: in the midst of writing this book, I joined Capital One Financial Corp., and was delighted to discover that Capital One comes closer to the ideal organization that I describe in *Build Your Castles in the Air* than anywhere else I've worked.

So here it is. I hope you enjoy and benefit from reading *Build Your Castles in the Air* as much as I enjoyed, and benefited from, compiling it.

Chuck Hansen

Foreword

By Nigel Morris
Co-Founder and former Chief Operating Officer and Vice Chairman
Capital One Financial Corp.

Thoreau didn't invent the principles of success that are in this book. He merely observed these principles at work around him—in nature, and in the nature of men—and gave them voice, literally setting words to the rhythm of the universe.

In the same way, I can't claim that in 1995 when my friend Rich Fairbank and I founded Capital One Financial Corporation, now a leading consumer finance company and a Fortune 200 corporation, we didn't consciously set out to follow the principles that Thoreau had captured in *Walden* and *Civil Disobedience*. We just knew—down deep, down in our bones—what we wanted the company to be, and we knew what we wanted the company *not* to be.

We knew that we wanted to create an organization that provided exceptional value to its investors, its customers and its associates. And at the same time, we knew that we wanted to create the type of environment that valued innovation, integrity, openness, teamwork, philanthropy, volunteerism and even fun.

We believed that the former would not truly be possible without the latter. As Maslow (and Thoreau) pointed out, before employees can embrace and achieve the strategic goals of an organization, they must first have met their most elemental physical, mental and emotional needs.

And what did we want the company *not* to be? Simply put, we didn't want it to be just another typical corporation. As consultants in the mid-1980s, we'd seen firsthand the deadly effects that corporate America's traditional, staid, stay-in-the-box thinking could have on employee morale and retention, innovation, customer service and, ultimately, on shareholder value.

In fact, it was during those days as consultants that Rich and I came up with the theory that became the core philosophy of Capital One. In a nutshell, we theorized that a bank could integrate the traditionally separate functions of marketing, credit, risk operations, and information technology to create a single flexible decision-making structure for assessing needs and assigning credit risk for each individual customer. By working backwards from the customer's needs and unique requirements, such a bank could offer a credit card product that was individually tailored to fit each customer.

We called this an information based strategy, or IBS. We believed that the first bank to adopt IBS in its credit card business would meet with great success, and we set out to find a bank willing to try.

But believe it or not, the idea of using information to tailor a credit card product—in that day of across-the-board 19.8% interest rate credit cards, regardless of individual credit risk or need—was so radical a concept that we had great difficulty convincing any bank of its value. We presented our idea to no fewer than 20 of the nation's largest banks before Signet, a regional bank based in Richmond, Va., agreed to take us on—provided Rich and I came on board to run the experiment.

We didn't realize it, but we were living out Thoreau's advice—*"advance confidently in the direction of your dreams, and endeavor to live the life which you have imagined"*—which Thoreau declared would result in *"success unexpected in common hours."*

And, in fact, Capital One was the very incarnation of "success unexpected in common hours"—and over the next eight years, it only got better. The company had grown from a division in a regional bank in 1988 to a start-up credit card company in 1995, and by 2002 we'd become a Fortune 200 financial services corporation with 17,000 associates, more than 45 million customers in markets all over the world, $17 billion in market capitalization, $10 billion in annual revenues, and one of the best financial performance records of any publicly traded company.

In retrospect, managing Capital One through this period of phenomenal growth seems rather like the Wright brothers' first airplane transforming itself into Spitfire high-performance aircraft, then into a jet plane, and finally into a rocket ship—all during that first flight!

We faced a steep learning curve with an abundance of peril. On one hand, it was critical to maintain some basic aerodynamic principles to keep the craft stable. On the other hand, we needed to look for opportunities to exploit the rapidly improving performance capabilities of the vehicle if we were to fulfill its potential.

As with the cultural characteristics with which we wished to imbue our company, many of the core principles that guided our decisions came not from our advanced business degrees, but from our gut, our hearts and our souls. It turns out that those ideas that we felt so deeply rang true for a reason: they were in fact, universal truths, and so many of them are captured in Thoreau's classic works.

And these universal truths made Capital One successful. Not only did we achieve Fortune 200 status, but we were named to the Fortune Magazine list of "America's 100 Best Companies to Work For" four times and the Sunday Times (UK) list of "Best Companies to Work For in the UK" four times (including a number three ranking in 2001), as well as similar lists in our site communities and in information technology and training publications.

And the core principle that we followed was the one from which the title of this book is drawn. Thoreau says it thus: *"If you have built castles in the air, your work need not be lost; that is where they should be. Now put the foundations under them."*

That is the story of Capital One, in a sentence. We built our castles in the air, we set audacious goals, we hung out our shingle proclaiming our intentions and then we worked to build the foundations underneath them. And I am proud to say we have so far succeeded.

In April, 2004, however, this story changed, as I began the next chapter in my life. I chose to leave Capital One, and for the first time since 1988, my life is not intertwined with the strategic planning and the day-to-day operations of this company. While I miss the excitement, the energy, and especially the people, I am enjoying pursuing new challenges and new rewards, not the least of which has been more time with my wife and family. I should not have been surprised to see that Thoreau had already captured my reasoning for this change:

I left the woods for as good a reason as I went there. Perhaps it seemed to me that I had several more lives to live, and could not spare any more time for that one. It is remarkable how easily and insensibly we fall into a particular route, and make a beaten track for ourselves.

As Chuck points out in the companion commentary to that quote: "Even the most ambitious and audacious plans can become routine and plain. You must continue to challenge yourself."

I have found comforting support for the way in which we built Capital One, and even for my decision to leave Capital One, all in the pages of this book. *Build Your Castles in the Air* is an engaging sampling of the brilliance of Thoreau and of his classic works, *Walden* and Civil Disobedience—both of which are surprisingly relevant to today's business world. Thoreau's philosophy, coupled with Chuck's insightful modern perspective, offers us a powerful guide and reference tool with a vital and authentic message.

Few other writers could have compiled this book. Chuck, like Thoreau, endeavors to live his life fully and on his own terms. Having adventured in the Caribbean, sailed across the North Atlantic, served as press secretary to a member of Congress, speechwriter to a Virginia governor and to Fortune 500 CEOs, and now as writer and motivational speaker, Chuck has embodied Thoreau's philosophy that we should fully participate in life: "*I did not wish to take a cabin passage, but rather to go before the mast and on the deck of the world...*"

I have experienced Thoreau's principles in action, both in business and in my life away from work. Chuck, in his commentary, offers further compelling witness to the power of Thoreau's remarkable approach to living one's life and to defining one's success.

I urge you to use this tool to live each day to the fullest, and on your own terms, and to experience the joy that this world offers each of us, if only we are willing to accept it.

Finding Your Calling

CHOOSE WISELY

When we consider what, to use the words of the catechism, is the chief end of man, and what are the true necessaries and means of life, it appears as if men had deliberately chosen the common mode of living because they preferred it to any other. Yet they honestly think there is no choice left. But alert and healthy natures remember that the sun rose clear. It is never too late to give up our prejudices.

There is always a choice regarding what to do with your life and with your career, and there is always enough time remaining to make that choice and take that action.

DISCOVER THE NEW WORLD WITHIN

"Direct your eye right inward, and you'll find A thousand regions in your mind Yet undiscovered. Travel them, and be Expert in home-cosmography."

What does Africa—what does the West stand for? Is not our own interior white on the chart?

Be rather the Mungo Park, the Lewis and Clark and Frobisher, of your own streams and oceans; explore your own higher latitudes—with shiploads of preserved meats to support you, if they be necessary; and pile the empty cans sky-high for a sign. Were preserved meats invented to preserve meat merely? Nay, be a Columbus to whole new continents and worlds within you, opening new channels, not of trade, but of thought. Every man is the lord of a realm beside which the earthly empire of the Czar is but a petty state, a hummock left by the ice.

If you are called to conquer Wall Street or Main Street, then so be it. But know that within you are resources and reserves that can make the conquest possible. Explore your mind, come to understand the strength you have inside, and you'll be infinitely better positioned to conquer the world outside.

DREAM, THEN LIVE YOUR DREAM

I learned this, at least, by my experiment: that if one advances confidently in the direction of his dreams, and endeavors to live the life which he has imagined, he will meet with a success unexpected in common hours. He will put some things behind, will pass an invisible boundary; new, universal, and more liberal laws will begin to establish themselves around and within him; or the old laws be expanded, and interpreted in his favor in a more liberal sense, and he will live with the license of a higher order of beings. In proportion as he simplifies his life, the laws of the universe will appear less complex, and solitude will not be solitude, nor poverty poverty, nor weakness weakness. If you have built castles in the air, your work need not be lost; that is where they should be. Now put the foundations under them.

This is the core of *Walden*, and one of the most important passages that I've ever read. Every sentence holds the wisdom of an MBA degree, a philosophy doctorate, a theology degree. Savor every word of *Walden* when you read it, but savor this paragraph most slowly and carefully.

EVERY DAY AN ADVENTURE

Men come tamely home at night only from the next field or street, where their house-hold echoes haunt, and their life pines because it breathes its own breath over again; their shadows, morning and evening, reach farther than their daily steps. We should come home from far, from adventures, and perils, and discoveries every day, with new experience and character.

Thoreau is not saying that you must climb Everest or cross Antarctica to gain this experience and character. After all, remember what Ralph Waldo Emerson said of Thoreau: "there was an excellent wisdom in him, proper to a rare class of men, which showed him the material world as a means and a symbol."

What Thoreau is saying is that even if you wake up every morning and walk down a single flight of stairs to your office or shop, it is possible to make every day an adventure, a learning experience, a journey of discovery. Examine every interaction you have with the natural world, as Thoreau did right down to watching the drama of life and death in an ant colony, and extract from it the jewels of experience and wisdom that God has left there for you to find.

FIND YOUR CALLING

To the sick the doctors wisely recommend a change of air and scenery....Yet we think that if rail fences are pulled down, and stone walls piled up on our farms, bounds are henceforth set to our lives and our fates decided. If you are chosen town clerk, forsooth, you cannot go to Tierra del Fuego this summer: but you may go to the land of infernal fire nevertheless. The universe is wider than our views of it. Yet we should oftener look over the tafferel of our craft, like curious passengers, and not make the voyage like stupid sailors picking oakum....Our voyaging is only great-circle sailing, and the doctors prescribe for diseases of the skin merely. One hastens to southern Africa to chase the giraffe; but surely that is not the game he would be after. How long, pray, would a man hunt giraffes if he could? Snipes and woodcocks also may afford rare sport; but I trust it would be nobler game to shoot one's self.

Three directionless years out of college, I bought a one-way ticket to St. Thomas, figuring if I was going to drift through life, I might as well drift on down to a tropical paradise. Seven months and many boat drinks and Caribbean adventures later, I had an epiphany sitting on a locals' topless beach, sipping a beer: I wasn't fulfilled. I had answered Thoreau's question: "How long, pray, would a man hunt giraffes if he could?" For me, it was seven months.

It begged another question: what was my calling? What could fulfill me if not living the life of St. Jimmy of the Caribbean? The answer turned out to be political communications. In my gut, I knew that's what I would be happy doing.

So I quit hunting giraffes and left the islands to embark on the journey toward my calling. Within three years, I was press secretary to a member of Congress. Since then I've served as communications director for the Virginia secretary of transportation and speechwriter to a Virginia governor.

My calling has changed since then, and I've tried to follow it faithfully, right up to this moment, as I work on my first book. The lesson remains with me: finding your calling, being the best at what in your heart you know you want to do, is the most powerful motivator of all—whether for yourself or your employees. Find self-actualization, as Maslow called it, and success, happiness and fulfillment will result.

POSSIBILITIES

John Farmer sat at his door one September evening, after a hard day's work, his mind still running on his labor more or less. Having bathed, he sat down to re-create his intellectual man. It was a rather cool evening, and some of his neighbors were apprehending a frost. He had not attended to the train of his thoughts long when he heard some one playing on a flute, and that sound harmonized with his mood. Still he thought of his work; but the burden of his thought was, that though this kept running in his head, and he found himself planning and contriving it against his will, yet it concerned him very little. It was no more than the scurf of his skin, which was constantly shuffled off. But the notes of the flute came home to his ears out of a different sphere from that he worked in, and suggested work for certain faculties which slumbered in him. They gently did away with the street, and the village, and the state in which he lived. A voice said to him—Why do you stay here and live this mean moiling life, when a glorious existence is possible for you? Those same stars twinkle over other fields than these.—But how to come out of this condition and actually migrate thither? All that he could think of was to practise some new austerity, to let his mind descend into his body and redeem it, and treat himself with ever increasing respect.

It is a valid question: "Why do you stay here and live this mean moiling life, when a glorious existence is possible for you?" But at the end of a long day, with the challenges of our work and our lives and all the demands that are upon us, it is a very hard question to get to.

John Farmer is on to something—perhaps some gentle music, a glass of wine on a porch swing, deep breathing and a view of the high-altitude cirrus clouds bypassing us and the troubles we face—it is possible to free your mind...to dream...to ask...

Why do you stay here and live this mean moiling life, when a glorious existence is possible for you?

POTENTIAL

I know of no more encouraging fact than the unquestionable ability of man to elevate his life by a conscious endeavor. It is something to be able to paint a particular picture, or to carve a statue, and so to make a few objects beautiful; but it is far more glorious to carve and paint the very atmosphere and medium through which we look, which morally we can do. To affect the quality of the day, that is the highest of arts. Every man is tasked to make his life, even in its details, worthy of the contemplation of his most elevated and critical hour.

Every new day is a lump of clay, a slab of stone. As you close your eyes at night, can you honestly say you've created the work of art that the day had the potential to become?

UNLIMITED CHOICES

So thoroughly and sincerely are we compelled to live, reverencing our life, and denying the possibility of change. This is the only way, we say; but there are as many ways as there can be drawn radii from one centre.

Too often we are like children driving motorized cars at the amusement park, the kind that follow a track along their course. We think we have only a small degree of latitude to steer left or right, and that the forests and fields to each side of our car are inaccessible to us. We believe our ultimate path is determined by the metal track below—our boss, our genetics, our socio-economic class, our education, our fears, our marriage(s) or our kids or luck or fate or…you get the point. By thinking this way, we make it true.

In fact we are four-wheel-drive trucks, and at any time—as long as we believe—we can jump the track and cut our own path. Success on this route is not certain, but you certainly will NOT find yourself, at the end of your life, having traveled a path you wouldn't have chosen if you had known you had a choice.

WHY WORK?

It is very evident what mean and sneaking lives many of you live, for my sight has been whetted by experience; always on the limits, trying to get into business and trying to get out of debt, a very ancient slough, called by the Latins aes alienum, another's brass, for some of their coins were made of brass; still living, and dying, and buried by this other's brass; always promising to pay, promising to pay, tomorrow, and dying today, insolvent; seeking to curry favor, to get custom, by how many modes, only not state-prison offenses; lying, flattering, voting, contracting yourselves into a nutshell of civility or dilating into an atmosphere of thin and vaporous generosity, that you may persuade your neighbor to let you make his shoes, or his hat, or his coat, or his carriage, or import his groceries for him; making yourselves sick, that you may lay up something against a sick day, something to be tucked away in an old chest, or in a stocking behind the plastering, or, more safely, in the brick bank; no matter where, no matter how much or how little.

What are you willing to give up for success? Independence? Dignity? Sincerity? Health?

In "It's My Job," Jimmy Buffett (and what book about a proper perspective on work would be complete without a reference to Brother Buffett?) sings about a happy street sweeper who teaches the singer a lesson about dignity in work, even in what would seem to be the very demeaning job of street sweeping.

What the street sweeper teaches us is that the issue is not that we work, or what we do for a living—the whole issue is: why do we do what we do? The person who cleans streets happily and well, because he has chosen this line of work freely and is committed to doing a good job, has more dignity than the person who has risen unhappily to the top level of the top corporation in a desperate attempt to meet the expectations of his neighbors, his parents, his wife or his in-laws.

WORK IS FUN (AT LEAST IT *CAN* BE)

Let not to get a living be thy trade, but thy sport.... Through want of enterprise and faith men are where they are, buying and selling, and spending their lives like serfs.

Not many people in this world are so well-off that they can choose not to work for a living. And by and large, the folks who must work are not happy about the situation—I'm sure you've heard the crack, "they call it work for a reason." But there are in fact people in this world who enjoy their jobs—whether out of passion for the type of activity or for the challenge of excelling in a given field or for other worthy reasons. But in general, enjoying your job strikes most people as the ultimate oxymoron.

Not long ago I traded my trusty, eight-year-old Isuzu Trooper and $500 for an eight-year-old Chrysler Sebring convertible (I like to say the car's color is "mid-life crisis gold"). Financially, it essentially was a wash (a car wash?)—I'll break even in a matter of months just in gas savings.

But the fact is, I didn't need a convertible. But my thinking was: as long as I'm going to own a car, why not make it a convertible, which I've always wanted?

Sounds like common sense, but it took a surprising amount of faith to make this leap. I'd been thinking about it for years, but for some reason, I'd always hesitated, frozen by a strange combination of fear and practicality.

I thought it was me until I started driving around in the new ragtop and friends started saying things like, "One day I'd like to get a convertible."

Many people look at work the same way. The idea of making a living doing something they enjoy seems impractical, frivolous and daring, all at the same time.

For me, though, the Sebring has come as a timely reminder about life and particularly about work. As long as you are going to have to work, why not make it a job you enjoy? Daring, revolutionary...and not really that hard to do, if you can summon the faith and the enterprise that Thoreau encourages.

Managing Your Day-to-Day Work

DELIBERATE

I delight to come to my bearings—not walk in procession with pomp and parade, in a conspicuous place, but to walk even with the Builder of the universe, if I may—not to live in this restless, nervous, bustling, trivial Nineteenth Century, but stand or sit thoughtfully while it goes by.

It's the difference between riding the whitewaters of the typical business day and sitting on the bank, watching the river rush by. Undeniably, to brave the rapids, frantically steering and paddling, crashing up against rocks and down over waterfalls, is exciting, and fun to do. But there is also reward to sitting on the bank and contemplating where the river begins and where it ends, and how it came to run by this spot, and what we are called to do within it. Time spent reflecting on these questions can bring us valuable perspective on the daily turbulence we endure, often by choice, out in the whitewaters of this restless, nervous, bustling, trivial Twenty-first Century.

EMAIL

For my part, I could easily do without the post-office. I think that there are very few important communications made through it.

In his essay about Napoleon, Ralph Waldo Emerson reports that the great general once directed that all letters be left unopened for three weeks, "and then observed with satisfaction how large a part of the correspondence had thus disposed of itself and no longer required an answer."

Hmm…

IMPERMANENCE OF OUR WORK

"Yes, we have done great deeds, and sung divine songs, which shall never die"—that is, as long as we can remember them. The learned societies and great men of Assyria—where are they?

At the end of this day, which of your actions has made the more significant impression: the perfectly crafted memo you fired off at work; or, the perfectly crafted story you gently weaved for your little girl at bedtime?

INCESSANT ANXIETY

Nature is as well adapted to our weakness as to our strength. The incessant anxiety and strain of some is a well-nigh incurable form of disease. We are made to exaggerate the importance of what work we do; and yet how much is not done by us! or, what if we had been taken sick? How vigilant we are! determined not to live by faith if we can avoid it; all the day long on the alert, at night we unwillingly say our prayers and commit ourselves to uncertainties.

The business will survive if you take a vacation this year. And you don't have to come in when you're sick. As a matter of fact, stay home, if you work in my office. A terminal hypochondriac, I don't need more reasons to believe how sick I already am. I've been to the hospital so many times for imagined diseases, they're giving me frequent liar miles. I get free upgrades to patient first class. I have my own plight attendant, and I'm sipping on an IV bag before most patients get their luggage stowed. I regularly hit the hospital on the way to vacations. And nothing says hypochondriac like a guy playing Frisbee on the beach with EKG patches shaved into his chest hair...

INCREASINGLY FASTER PACE OF LIFE

Have not men improved somewhat in punctuality since the railroad was invented? Do they not talk and think faster in the depot than they did in the stage-office?

I think it's fascinating that, in any given community, the speed at which automatic doors open and close often is approximately calibrated to the pace of life there (although I haven't checked if this is an urban legend). Thus one's speed of thought and action are tied to a place's pace of technology and of life—you must think and act more quickly to enter a New York City elevator than a Richmond, Virginia elevator (in the comparatively rare cases in which you use an elevator here). I've also noticed Washington, D.C. escalators are faster than those in Richmond, and that riders in D.C. speed up their journey by climbing the stairs, even as the stairs carry them upward.

Interestingly, in this quote, Thoreau does not imply that faster—whether in elevator doors or the pace of life—is better or worse. In my experience, though, each of us can find a happy medium, in our work and in our lives.

INFORMATION CULTURE

To a philosopher all news, as it is called, is gossip, and they who edit and read it are old women over their tea.

INFORMATION CULTURE (II)

Hardly a man takes a half-hour's nap after dinner, but when he wakes he holds up his head and asks, "What's the news?" as if the rest of mankind had stood his sentinels...

Initially, I wrote some pithy commentary for these quotes that referenced the Internet and all-news networks, and in the process missed the applicable business lesson.

Quote one asserts that, to a philosopher, all news is simply gossip, and seems to imply that higher-minded individuals need not bother themselves with such tittle-tattle. Quote two questions the value of constantly asking "what's the news?"

But Thoreau's question does not make it any less true that human beings constantly seek out information about topics that are important to them. Here's the problem: a philosopher-manager who feels she is above satisfying employees' constant appetite for information, or lowering herself to compete with the sources of gossip that her employees are listening to, is abdicating her communication responsibilities.

Employees will seek out information about executive office maneuverings, buy outs, acquisitions, SEC investigations, etc., if only to exert some small measure of control in an otherwise uncontrollable world. If the manager deigns not to communicate, employees will seek information elsewhere—from the grapevine, the media, or even (yikes!) from the Yahoo! message boards.

"Communicate too much" has become a trendy management philosophy, but most employees will tell you that the corner offices "communicate too much" only about the unimportant and the positive, and communicate too little about the important or the negative.

INNOVATION

The migrating buffalo, which seeks new pastures in another latitude, is not extravagant like the cow which kicks over the pail, leaps the cowyard fence, and runs after her calf, in milking time.

The good news for individuals (or organizations) who are not now innovative is that even the smallest steps forward represent quantum leaps. The bad news is that it may take a quantum leap in imagination to understand that these tiny steps are even possible.

INTENTION V. ACTION

…Nor need the soldier be so idle as to try to paint the precise color of his virtue on his standard. The enemy will find it out. He may turn pale when the trial comes.

Companies try to paint the precise color of their virtue on their standard when they spend dozens (hundreds? thousands?) of hours smithing the words of their mission statement.

But these statements are only worth the actions that back them. When the trial comes—and in my experience, that trial occurs every day, in the big and especially the little decisions—we will truly demonstrate our virtue.

THE INTERNET'S POWER

If we live in the Nineteenth Century, why should we not enjoy the advantages which the Nineteenth Century offers? Why should our life be in any respect provincial? If we will read newspapers, why not skip the gossip of Boston and take the best newspaper in the world at once?—not be sucking the pap of "neutral family" papers, or browsing "Olive Branches" here in New England. Let the reports of all the learned societies come to us, and we will see if they know anything. Why should we leave it to Harper & Brothers and Redding & Co. to select our reading?

I included this quote as a testament to the power of the Internet—a power that we should harness regularly. It also is a testament to the power of the mind of Henry David Thoreau.

KILLING TIME

Think, also, of the ladies of the land weaving toilet cushions against the last day, not to betray too green an interest in their fates! As if you could kill time without injuring eternity.

We spend tremendous amounts of energy denying to ourselves our own mortality, focusing resolutely on the comparatively insignificant work of this world and of this day. If we channeled that energy toward improving ourselves, how much better prepared would we be, not only for eternity, but for the inevitabilities of this world: forced career changes, mid-life crises, retirement, or even just tomorrow? This is not a "life philosophy" issue so much as it is a day-to-day issue that we should constantly be addressing, many times a day, with each little decision we make regarding how best to spend the next minute of our lives.

LITTLE STEPS

For it matters not how small the beginning may seem to be: what is once well done is done forever. (CD)

My wife, Stacy, is blessed with an 90-year-old grandfather, Bingo. I am blessed as well—in the 14 years I've known Bingo, I have learned a great deal from him. One of Bingo's most enduring lessons came after my brother Ken tag-teamed with gravity to shatter a plank on the steps leading to the basement.

The next day when I got home from work, Bingo was already down in the basement, moving slowly around the damaged stairway with tools and a piece of lumber. One of our cats, Abbott, sat nearby, watching Bingo intently. I decided I'd join Abbott and sat down on a dusty old stool.

After just a few moments, I knew I'd better get comfortable. Bingo was moving with purpose and direction, but not with much velocity. For a modern man like myself, accustomed to microwaved meals and high-speed computers and pre-fabricated pretty-much everything, watching Bingo shuffle and stoop around the stairway in his work was quite difficult. I was certain we would be there until 9 p.m. at least.

So Abbott and I sat and watched while Bingo worked. Bingo's movements were fascinating—he never seemed to rush, but he also never seemed to stop moving. Every action was deliberate, and no action was superfluous, as he removed the broken old step, measured and cut the new board to length, put the board precisely in place and nailed it down securely. Each tiny task linked directly to the task before and the task following, and they quickly formed a deceptively swift train of action.

Before I could get comfortable on the old stool, Bingo was gathering up his tools and sweeping the sawdust from the floor, and the stairway was better than new.

In our hectic world, it is often difficult to find our way to completion on our most important tasks. But what Bingo taught Abbott and me that day is that deliberate actions—even small ones—done well and done consistently, will get you to your destination, often far sooner than you might expect.

MORALITY AND GOODNESS

Our whole life is startlingly moral. There is never an instant's truce between virtue and vice. Goodness is the only investment that never fails. In the music of the harp which trembles round the world it is the insisting on this which thrills us. The harp is the travelling patterer for the Universe's Insurance Company, recommending its laws, and our little goodness is all the assessment that we pay. Though the youth at last grows indifferent, the laws of the universe are not indifferent, but are forever on the side of the most sensitive. Listen to every zephyr for some reproof, for it is surely there, and he is unfortunate who does not hear it.

Think of the harp melody that Thoreau describes as satellite radio for your soul. No matter where you go this timeless music can resonate within you, as long as you have your receiver with you and tuned in. This should inform every single decision you make every single day.

NEGLECTING LIFE'S FINER FRUITS

Most men, even in this comparatively free country, through mere ignorance and mistake, are so occupied with the factitious cares and superfluously coarse labors of life that its finer fruits cannot be plucked by them. Their fingers, from excessive toil, are too clumsy and tremble too much for that. Actually, the laboring man has not leisure for a true integrity day by day; he cannot afford to sustain the manliest relations to men; his labor would be depreciated in the market. He has no time to be anything but a machine....The finest qualities of our nature, like the bloom on fruits, can be preserved only by the most delicate handling. Yet we do not treat ourselves nor one another thus tenderly.

How many times have you spent a hard day working to provide for your family, only to come home so torqued up and worried that you could not focus your full attention and joy upon them—and then they were asleep, and another day, another chance, had slipped away? How many times have you thought to call a friend and then did not, too busy with life's fractious cares for a ten-minute conversation? Do your fingers tremble too much to embrace the ones you love, to pluck these finer fruits of life?

PRODUCTIVE IDLENESS

I have spent many an hour, when I was younger, floating over its surface as the zephyr willed, having paddled my boat to the middle, and lying on my back across the seats, in a summer forenoon, dreaming awake, until I was aroused by the boat touching the sand, and I arose to see what shore my fates had impelled me to; days when idleness was the most attractive and productive industry.

My brother Ken, no mean philosopher himself, likes to ask: When was the last time you watched a cloud go from one horizon to the other? There is value in taking time to reflect, to remove yourself from the chaos of your day-to-day life and allow that din to subside. Once you've quieted all the external noise, you can, listening carefully, begin to hear to the song of your soul, which should serve as your compass as you make those day-to-day business decisions.

SIMPLICITY, SIMPLICITY, SIMPLICITY

Our life is frittered away by detail. An honest man has hardly need to count more than his ten fingers, or in extreme cases he may add his ten toes, and lump the rest. Simplicity, simplicity, simplicity! I say, let your affairs be as two or three, and not a hundred or a thousand; instead of a million count half a dozen, and keep your accounts on your thumb-nail.

Know when to say no—"No" to off-strategy business objectives, "No" to out-of-scope requests of your department, "No" to over-the-transom work that crowds out the most strategically important items on your daily to-do list. Do a handful of few important tasks well, not a hundred unimportant tasks poorly.

STAYING FOCUSED IN DAILY CHAOS

Let us spend one day as deliberately as Nature, and not be thrown off the track by every nutshell and mosquito's wing that falls on the rails. Let us rise early and fast, or break fast, gently and without perturbation; let company come and let company go, let the bells ring and the children cry—determined to make a day of it. Why should we knock under and go with the stream? Let us not be upset and overwhelmed in that terrible rapid and whirlpool called a dinner, situated in the meridian shallows. Weather this danger and you are safe, for the rest of the way is down hill. With unrelaxed nerves, with morning vigor, sail by it, looking another way, tied to the mast like Ulysses. If the engine whistles, let it whistle till it is hoarse for its pains. If the bell rings, why should we run?

The modern workday seems to be nothing more than a string of interruptions of interruptions. How many times have you started the day with a plan, only to spend the entire day dealing with the issue raised in your first email or voicemail? Thoreau says stand firm in the stream of distractions, focus on your goal and make a day of it. Or in the immortal words of Gold Five to the Rebel X-Wing pilot at the end of "Star Wars": "Stay on target! Stay on target!!"

STRATEGY

There were scores of pitch pines around my house, from one to four inches in diameter, which had been gnawed by mice the previous winter—a Norwegian winter for them, for the snow lay long and deep, and they were obliged to mix a large proportion of pine bark with their other diet. These trees were alive and apparently flourishing at midsummer, and many of them had grown a foot, though completely girdled; but after another winter such were without exception dead. It is remarkable that a single mouse should thus be allowed a whole pine tree for its dinner, gnawing round instead of up and down it...

A task or problem of any size can be handled provided you choose the right angle of attack—a single mouse can kill a 4-inch pine tree simply by gnawing a ring around its base.

TECHNOLOGY

We do not ride on the railroad; it rides upon us.

This for me is one of Thoreau's most powerful, valuable insights. Albert Einstein once said that "Technological progress is like an axe in the hands of a pathological criminal."

Think about that the next time a technological "innovation" makes it possible for you (followed quickly by your boss demanding you) to do more faster—or to work while you are at home, on vacation, in airplanes, even on the little league diamond. Are you riding upon technology, or is it riding upon you?

THEORY V. ACTION

There are nowadays professors of philosophy, but not philosophers…To be a philosopher is not merely to have subtle thoughts, nor even to found a school, but so to love wisdom as to live according to its dictates, a life of simplicity, independence, magnanimity, and trust. It is to solve some of the problems of life, not only theoretically, but practically.

The easy approach on this quote is to use it as an indictment of outside consultants…the proverbial experts on childrearing who don't have kids of their own (to paraphrase a popular but slightly risqué take on the consulting profession).

As always, though, it is much more useful, and difficult, to apply the lesson to yourself; which is: You must live your ideals day-in and day-out, or they are not truly ideals, but meaningless musings.

UNENDING WORK

I have travelled a good deal in Concord; and everywhere, in shops, and offices, and fields, the inhabitants have appeared to me to be doing penance in a thousand remarkable ways....The twelve labors of Hercules were trifling in comparison with those which my neighbors have undertaken; for they were only twelve, and had an end; but I could never see that these men slew or captured any monster or finished any labor. They have no friend Iolaus to burn with a hot iron the root of the hydra's head, but as soon as one head is crushed, two spring up.

To what end are you pursuing endless labor? How will you know you're done? As the saying goes, no one dies with an empty inbox...

WORK DOESN'T HAVE TO BE WORK

By avarice and selfishness, and a grovelling habit, from which none of us is free, of regarding the soil as property, or the means of acquiring property chiefly, the landscape is deformed, husbandry is degraded with us, and the farmer leads the meanest of lives. He knows Nature but as a robber.

While earning my masters degree in public relations and public affairs in San Francisco, I also sought out work, concentrating on PR and advertising. During the search a forty-something PR guy granted me an informational interview—he had no job to offer but was happy to share his story of success in the industry. After hearing him describe a typical day writing and creating and communicating, I couldn't contain my excitement. "It must be so cool to get paid for doing this!" I gushed.

A strange, almost disoriented look fell over the PR pro's face. "Yeah, I suppose," he said slowly, then paused, as if he'd suddenly found himself lost. "I guess…," he said, then paused again. "I guess it's just sort of…become a job."

WORK

I would not be one of those who will foolishly drive a nail into mere lath and plastering; such a deed would keep me awake nights. Give me a hammer, and let me feel for the furring. Do not depend on the putty. Drive a nail home and clinch it so faithfully that you can wake up in the night and think of your work with satisfaction—a work at which you would not be ashamed to invoke the Muse. So will help you God, and so only. Every nail driven should be as another rivet in the machine of the universe, you carrying on the work.

Do good and meaningful work.

Managing Your Career

BREAK OUT

I left the woods for as good a reason as I went there. Perhaps it seemed to me that I had several more lives to live, and could not spare any more time for that one. It is remarkable how easily and insensibly we fall into a particular route, and make a beaten track for ourselves. I had not lived there a week before my feet wore a path from my door to the pond-side; and though it is five or six years since I trod it, it is still quite distinct. It is true, I fear, that others may have fallen into it, and so helped to keep it open. The surface of the earth is soft and impressible by the feet of men; and so with the paths which the mind travels. How worn and dusty, then, must be the highways of the world, how deep the ruts of tradition and conformity!

Even the most ambitious and audacious plans can become routine and plain. You must continue to challenge yourself.

CAREER MANAGEMENT

I am wont to think that men are not so much the keepers of herds as herds are the keepers of men, the former are so much the freer.

Are you shepherding your career, or is your career shepherding you?

(Hint—which part of your anatomy comes in contact most often with the shepherd's staff—your hand or your rear end?)

EARNED SUCCESS

I do not suppose that I have attained to obscurity, but I should be proud if no more fatal fault were found with my pages on this score than was found with the Walden ice. Southern customers objected to its blue color, which is the evidence of its purity, as if it were muddy, and preferred the Cambridge ice, which is white, but tastes of weeds.

Did you know that SPAM recently made a comeback, this time as fashionable cuisine? Nothing against those fine folks out on the farm who work sun up to sun down raising…uh,…cows, or spows, or spork, or what ever animal those square globs of meat come from…But the fact that SPAM came to be considered high-fashion food should be the ultimate demonstration that anyone who allows a boss or neighbors or family members or society or even the culinary fashion elite to validate their own success—well, why not?—may have SPAM for brains.

IMAGINE A SIMPLER LIFE

If he and his family would live simply, they might all go a-huckleberrying in the summer for their amusement. John heaved a sigh at this, and his wife stared with arms a-kimbo, and both appeared to be wondering if they had capital enough to begin such a course with, or arithmetic enough to carry it through. It was sailing by dead reckoning to them, and they saw not clearly how to make their port so; therefore I suppose they still take life bravely, after their fashion, face to face, giving it tooth and nail, not having skill to split its massive columns with any fine entering wedge, and rout it in detail;—thinking to deal with it roughly, as one should handle a thistle. But they fight at an overwhelming disadvantage—living, John Field, alas! without arithmetic, and failing so.

So many of us create the circumstances ourselves that require us to live hand to mouth, scrambling and scrapping for every dollar, goaded by expectations imposed upon us by ourselves and by others, and hounded by the debts we've accumulated while establishing our complicated lives—all the while dreaming in vain of a simpler life that we don't realize could be ours if we would just give up the race. Sit down and really do the math. It is possible.

LIVING TO WORK, OR WORKING TO LIVE?

But men labor under a mistake. The better part of the man is soon plowed into the soil for compost. By a seeming fate, commonly called necessity, they are employed, as it says in an old book, laying up treasures which moth and rust will corrupt and thieves break through and steal. It is a fool's life, as they will find when they get to the end of it, if not before.

Not long ago, my wife and I rolled the dice and purchased mail-order pets for the educational benefit of our children. These were a colony of ants of southwestern United States extraction ("DO NOT release your ants; they are not native to most of America and DO NOT have a role in your local ecosystem!") that arrived in our mailbox in the heat of June.

Once in their new home, a pebbly moonscape built around a plastic mound too steep by half, our ants hurled themselves into their labors, spending their brief time on Earth working like dogs to build a semi-elaborate tunnel system. For hours, we'd watch with our 7-year-old son and 5-year-old daughter as the ants struggled toward the top of the hill with a huge boulder in their jaws, only to lose their footing (often thanks to a bump from a colleague) and tumble hundreds of ant-stories down to the rocky bottom of the container.

As foreshadowed in the instructions, however, within three weeks of their arrival, the pitiful carcasses of the once energetic go-getters lay strewn across their life's work, in some cases still gripping a pebble in their pinchers. It reminded me of the guy who works day and night and weekends too at a widget company, clawing his way to vice president, and then dies, and his obituary headline reads not "Father of three dies" or "Devoted husband dies" or "Man who tried to find meaning in life dies." Instead, the obit headline reads: "Widget executive dies" and somehow, even in death, the workaholic's obsession overpowers all other facets of his life.

PERSONAL GOALS

In the long run men hit only what they aim at. Therefore, though they should fail immediately, they had better aim at something high.

This may look like a no-brainer, but it's tricky. I absolutely agree: aim high. Build your castles in the air, then put the foundations under them. But take care not to frame goals that stake your success to factors you can't control. This is where I think some self-development experts have unintentionally misled us, with their mantra of "dream it and you can be it..."

This may be heresy, but I don't believe that. I believe that if you can dream it, you can focus all your power on making it happen, and thereby maximize your chances for achieving the dream. I also deeply believe in Thoreau's advice that if one "advances confidently in the direction of his dreams, and endeavors to live the life which he has imagined, he will meet with a success unexpected in common hours."

But you can't, with 100% certainty, build events you can't control into your plans, any more than you can build future lottery winnings into your financial plans.

Let me try another example: Bob Dole. Dole tried and failed three times to become president. Regardless, he is a former senator, former congressman, elder statesman, war hero and role model for millions of disabled and fully-abled alike. Should Dole consider himself a failure for not achieving the presidency?

Of course not! Becoming president involves a myriad uncontrollable factors, from your opponent's actions to the decisions of tens of millions of voters. Dole's goal should have been (and might have been) to do everything in his power to be elected president. As long as did that, he is not a failure.

Yes, aim high. But recognize what is in your control, and what is not. Pledge to do everything in your power to accomplish a goal—then specify those necessary actions and do them. The result will be a life marked more by satisfaction than by quiet desperation, and the odds will improve that you will achieve—and believe you have achieved—your optimum potential in life.

POSSESSIONS

Cultivate poverty like a garden herb, like sage. Do not trouble yourself much to get new things, whether clothes or friends. Turn the old; return to them. Things do not change; we change. Sell your clothes and keep your thoughts.

I've been thinking lately about work-life balance. Many of us say we are working too long, too hard, missing out on time with our families, for ourselves. And I think it's true: businesses have progressively asked for more and more from their employees, prompting calls for more work-life balance.

But here's the thing: work-life balance is just that—a balance. Want more time away from work? Simply find a job that gives you that kind of time.

"Wait!" you say. "All those positions pay far less than I can live on!" And that's the core problem: we create lives for ourselves that require high-paying jobs—sometimes two such jobs in the same household—to maintain. Plasma TVs, expensive new SUVs, super-sized houses, pricey convenience goods, unlimited toys for the kids, maxed out credit cards…these are why we need to work so hard and so long.

But then we tell our employers that we expect to keep the high salaries we require while working fewer hours. We are asking for our cake and eating it too, in oversized portions.

If you are serious, really serious, about achieving work-life balance, the most effective variable you can address in the equation is lifestyle. Buy less stuff. Learn to live with less. It's actually pretty simple.

Face it: it's not the company's fault you're financially over-extended. If you're not getting enough time with your kids, it's possible you should chalk that up to an overly lavish lifestyle that forces you to work longer and harder, and prevents you from exploring other options, like reduced hours or getting a different job.

Your lifestyle is the first variable to address, and it will give you more flexibility to find the job that you really want with the hours that you really want to work. It's a hard truth—but it's still true. It also is true that I do not practice what I preach on this one. But at least now I'm thinking about it.

PRINCIPLE MINUS ACTION EQUALS...WHAT?

How can a man be satisfied to entertain and opinion merely, and enjoy it? Is there any enjoyment in it, if his opinion is that he is aggrieved? If you are cheated out of a single dollar by your neighbor, you do not rest satisfied with knowing you are cheated, or with saying that you are cheated, or even with petitioning him to pay you your due; but you take effectual steps at once to obtain the full amount, and see to it that you are never cheated again. Action from principle, the perception and the performance of right, changes things and relations; it is essentially revolutionary, and does not consist wholly with anything which was. (CD)

The fiber of a person's character is strengthened with each principle-based proactive action he or she takes.

And not only is the person taking action transformed, but that person's fundamental relationship with the situation and with life is revolutionized. Longfellow once wrote that in this world, man is either hammer or anvil. Do you act upon the world, or does the world act upon you?

STATUS HOMES

...A man has no more to do with the style of architecture of his house than a tortoise with that of its shell...What of architectural beauty I now see, I know has gradually grown from within outward, out of the necessities and character of the indweller, who is the only builder—out of some unconscious truthfulness, and nobleness, without ever a thought for the appearance and whatever additional beauty of this kind is destined to be produced will be preceded by a like unconscious beauty of life.

Much has been made about the fact that the average square footage of new homes today is much higher than it was in past generations. Likewise, the stuff that we fill these houses with have become more elaborate and expensive, from big-screen televisions to high-tech kitchen gadgets to piles and piles of electronic toys (which, of course, create the need to work longer and longer hours to be able to purchase this lifestyle).

Yet, despite bigger homes and all that comes with them, many people are falling short of fulfillment. Could it be that we are demanding larger and larger houses to hold the increasing emptiness that we feel?

SUCCESS

Some are dinning in our ears that we Americans, and moderns generally, are intellectual dwarfs compared with the ancients, or even the Elizabethan men. But what is that to the purpose? A living dog is better than a dead lion. Shall a man go and hang himself because he belongs to the race of pygmies, and not be the biggest pygmy that he can? Let every one mind his own business, and endeavor to be what he was made.

Compare yourself not to history, not to others, and not even to yourself, but to what you could be.

WEALTH

Superfluous wealth can buy superfluities only.

Additional commentary here would be superfluous.

WHOSE TIME IS IT ANYWAY?

*Some of you, we all know, are poor, find it hard to live, are sometimes, as it were,
gasping for breath. I have no doubt that some of you who read this book are unable to
pay for all the dinners which you have actually eaten, or for the coats and shoes which
are fast wearing or are already worn out, and have come to this page to spend bor-
rowed or stolen time, robbing your creditors of an hour.*

In Parker Brothers' board game "Life," you receive a certain amount of money
at the beginning of the game, and the object is to use it wisely, and to spend it on
the right things, in order to win.

In the real game of life, we begin with an unknowable allotment of a different
currency: time. We do not know how much we've been given, and once spent, it
cannot be recovered—time passed is time past. But how we spend our time
today, and how and to whom we decide to commit our time in the future, is
within our control.

Live simply, spend modestly, enter into debt cautiously, and you are doing
more than saving money. You are promising your current and future time to
yourself and your own purposes, rather mortgaging your lifetime of time allotted
to creditors and employers.

In Luke 19:11 in the Bible, Jesus tells his disciples of the master who, before
going on a trip, gave his servants ten minas each to invest, to put to work. When
the master returned, he smiled upon the servants who had used this gift wisely,
and punished the servant who had not.

We choose our lifestyle, for the most part, and in doing so, we choose how we
will spend the time we've been granted.

Managing The Business

BUSINESS ADVICE

The modern cheap and fertile press, with all its translations, has done little to bring us nearer to the heroic writers of antiquity.

   The Internet and bookshelves sing with a cacophony of business "wisdom." Yet few strike the chords that resonate with timeless truths. Whether from this book or some other source, don't accept theories and statements of certainty without examination.

COMMON SENSE

The broadest and most prevalent error requires the most disinterested virtue to sustain it. (CD)

COMMON SENSE IS TOO COMMON

Why level downward to our dullest perception always, and praise that as common sense? The commonest sense is the sense of men asleep, which they express by snoring.

Voltaire said that "Common sense is the least common of the senses." He and Thoreau do not necessarily disagree. Thoreau condemns the idiocy that passes as wisdom when we refuse to think; Voltaire laments the absence of thinking that would make real common sense more common.

CONVENTIONAL WISDOM

Shams and delusions are esteemed for soundest truths, while reality is fabulous.

This passage is about the folly of conventional wisdom, which can be passed down through the generations, passed on as "news" or "analysis," or passed off by so-called "experts." Compare to reality the many predictions made by the economic and political experts, and the folly of conventional wisdom and the opinions of those "in the know" becomes clear.

No life, and no business, should start from scratch in its learning about the way the world works, but instead build on the truths learned by others and over the ages. The trick is to select the learnings that are genuinely true, and discard those which are simply institutionalized negativity. In the end, you must trust yourself to make the correct distinctions.

CORPORATE CULTURE

I was not born to be forced. I will breathe after my own fashion. Let us see who is the strongest. What force has a multitude? They only can force me who obey a higher law than I. They force me to become like themselves. I do not hear of men being forced to live this way or that by masses of men. What sort of life were that to live? (CD)

You shape the corporate culture, not the other way around.

CORPORATE GOALS

I cannot believe that our factory system is the best mode by which men may get clothing. The condition of the operatives is becoming every day more like that of the English; and it cannot be wondered at, since, as far as I have heard or observed, the principal object is, not that mankind may be well and honestly clad, but, unquestionably, that corporations may be enriched.

Shoddy products and high profits may be the short-term result of this thinking, but a shoddy reputation and a deterioration of the business' integrity are the long-term results. The negative effect is magnified in inverse proportion to the period over which the goals are expected to be achieved, and long-term success is impossible in a culture that demands steady, constant quarter-to-quarter or month-to-month increases in profit.

CORPORATE RESPONSIBILITY

It is truly enough said that a corporation has no conscience; but a corporation of conscientious men is a corporation with a conscience. (CD)

Corporate America gets a bad rap. At the three Fortune 500 companies where I've worked, I've found the vast majority of men and women do indeed have a conscience, and they often are willing to make brave stands to stop an injustice from being committed—even, and especially in some cases, up in the oft-maligned executive suites.

On top of that, I have yet to work for a large corporation or organization that was well organized enough to pull off the prevalent conspiracy theories. It's hard enough just to get the plan put together for the next year, much less infuse every part of that plan with the elements of a sinister plot.

In my experience, when organizations do fail the test of conscientious action, it is usually the result of one of three circumstances:

1. Non-existent "pressure" from leadership to accept a bad idea—I've often seen employees assume that leadership doesn't want to hear about problems. But in truth, leaders are in fact receptive to *constructively presented* red flags (criticism that comes with solution options—don't tell they why it *shouldn't* be done; tell them *how* it *can* be done).

2. Rush rush rush—Today's employees are overwhelmed. Six-month plans are overrun and made irrelevant by day-to-day crises, and best intentions drown amid a rising sea of voicemails, emails and instant messages. In this environment, little things and not-so-little things fall through the cracks. Later, in the suspicious light of hindsight, these mistakes can seem sinister and premeditated, but I don't believe most are.

3. Little losses—Here we actually see conscious wrong-doing, albeit in small doses. Little losses are conscious decisions to do the wrong thing, which is usually the easiest thing on a seemingly inconsequential matter. Over time, these little losses add up to a pattern of wrong-doing by the employee and by the company. The thousands of little decisions we make weekly come together to define the kind of person we are, and the kind of company we're a part of. This is where the employee with a con-

science can do some of his best work, even if in a small way, providing the company with the internal moral compass it must have.

EVOLUTION

This American government—what is it but a tradition, though a recent one, endeavoring to transmit itself unimpaired to posterity, but each instant losing some of its integrity? (CD)

Setting aside for now the point Thoreau is making about government, let's look at this quote as it relates to any organization, including a business. Many times, a business is born and nurtured from a idealistic, passion-inspiring vision. Working in this environment can be heady, invigorating and emotionally rewarding.

But over time, as the business expands, new folks join, institutional memory leaves or fades, and the day-to-day work begins to dominate decisions and activities, the original, idealistic vision, and the passionate culture it inspired, begins to wane.

Thoreau warns us against this phenomenon. Simply by being aware that it can happen, we can be alert to the signs of the decay of that founding culture and vision, and work to retain the most desirable of these traits.

EXPANSION—SIDE ONE

What was the meaning of that South-Sea Exploring Expedition, with all its parade and expense, but an indirect recognition of the fact that there are continents and seas in the moral world to which every man is an isthmus or an inlet, yet unexplored by him, but that it is easier to sail many thousand miles through cold and storm and cannibals, in a government ship, with five hundred men and boys to assist one, than it is to explore the private sea, the Atlantic and Pacific Ocean of one's being alone.

This has double applicability. For individuals, it warns against taking the easier path of outward exploration while neglecting to explore one's inner worlds.

For companies, it is an equally cautionary comment about global expansion. Remember this obsequious phrase from the '90s?: "if we could get a [insert product here] to every Chinese consumer…" Yet, many exotic markets turned out as barren as the Antarctic landscape—and profit was inversely proportional to the resources spent planting the company flag there. Meanwhile, our boring domestic market flourished, as did companies who "stuck to their knitting," staying focused on their loyal customers in their established markets.

EXPANSION—SIDE TWO

It is not worth the while to go round the world to count the cats in Zanzibar. Yet do this even till you can do better, and you may perhaps find some "Symmes' Hole" by which to get at the inside at last.

The flip side of the previous argument is that if one focused only on one's own backyard, distant markets will never be discovered. Somewhere between foolish navel-gazing and foolish naval expeditions is a moderate, measured, deliberate approach to expansion that holds the most promise.

INNOVATION

It is a ridiculous demand which England and America make, that you shall speak so that they can understand you. Neither men nor toadstools grow so. As if that were important, and there were not enough to understand you without them. As if Nature could support but one order of understandings, could not sustain birds as well as quadrupeds, flying as well as creeping things, and hush and whoa, which Bright can understand, were the best English. As if there were safety in stupidity alone. I fear chiefly lest my expression may not be extravagant enough, may not wander far enough beyond the narrow limits of my daily experience, so as to be adequate to the truth of which I have been convinced.

Too often in organizations, innovative approaches to problems or opportunities are spiked for the cardinal offense of "not the way we do it here." Demanding that research and innovative thought follow a predetermined path to a pre-approved destination is like demanding that a river follow a set path to a set opening to the ocean. The only way to keep a river in the officially sanctioned riverbed is to reduce the volume of water, leaving it too anemic to break its banks. Research and development is much the same.

LUXURY'S DISTRACTIONS

Moreover, if you are restricted in your range by poverty, if you cannot buy books and newspapers, for instance, you are but confined to the most significant and vital experiences; you are compelled to deal with the material which yields the most sugar and the most starch. It is life near the bone where it is sweetest.

I work for a company that is famous for its beautiful facilities, well-equipped fitness centers, inviting meeting spaces and fun culture. In many ways, my company resembles the now-defunct dot-coms. But from my perspective, there is a difference: the first order of business is to generate consistent profits and return on investment for shareholders over the long-term. The great place to work stuff is a way to attract and retain the talent that can achieve the main goal. The dot-coms, on the other hand, seemed to be about the work experience first, and the bottom line second, if at all. If they'd focused less on distracting "benefits" such as plush corporate facilities, pinball machines and game rooms, would they have been compelled to focus their attentions on those activities yielding "the most sugar and the most starch"—that is, profitable activities?

A MORAL WORKPLACE

Confucius says truly, "Virtue does not remain as an abandoned orphan; it must of necessity have neighbors."

Stand, alone, if you must, in your integrity. You will not be alone for long.

NARROW-MINDFULNESS

What youthful philosophers and experimentalists we are! There is not one of my readers who has yet lived a whole human life. These may be but the spring months in the life of the race. If we have had the seven-years' itch, we have not seen the seventeen-year locust yet in Concord. We are acquainted with a mere pellicle of the globe on which we live. Most have not delved six feet beneath the surface, nor leaped as many above it. We know not where we are.

All this is to say: know what you don't know. It is easy to dismiss new ideas with the excuse that "we've already tried that" or "that's not the way we do it," citing bad past experiences as proof. Thoreau warns that we do not know how much of the total world we've already seen—either the physical world or the business world. Therefore, we should be careful about what lessons we draw from the narrow slice of the world we have experienced.

But there also is a more optimistic side to this passage: if the small slice of the world and creation that we've experiences is as breathtaking and amazing as it is, imagine how wonderful the whole must be!

New Economy

It is said that the British Empire is very large and respectable, and that the United States are a first-rate power. We do not believe that a tide rises and falls behind every man which can float the British Empire like a chip, if he should ever harbor it in his mind. Who knows what sort of seventeen-year locust will next come out of the ground? The government of the world I live in was not framed, like that of Britain, in after-dinner conversations over the wine.

The laws of economics are as basic and constant as the law of gravity, and are as difficult to bend or break. Consider with skepticism those dinner party pundits who claim that a man-made technology or industry has created a new order in which the basic laws of economics are obsolete. A business must still make money to survive, no matter how cool its web site.

PETER PRINCIPLE

But the rich man—not to make any invidious comparison—is always sold to the institution which makes him rich. Absolutely speaking, the more money, the less virtue; for money comes between a man and his objects, and obtains them for him; it was certainly no great virtue to obtain it. It puts to rest many questions which he would otherwise be taxed to answer; while the only new question which it puts is the hard but superfluous one, how to spend it. Thus his moral ground is taken from under his feet. The opportunities of living are diminished in proportion as that are called the "means" are increased. The best thing a man can do for his culture when he is rich is to endeavor to carry out those schemes which he entertained when he was poor. (CD)

A variation of this made the email rounds recently:
If: (Knowledge = Power) and (Time = Money)
And physics dictates that: (Work = Power x Time),
Then: (Work = Knowledge x Money).
Solving for Money: (Money = Work/Knowledge).
Therefore, as Knowledge approaches zero, Money increases, regardless of how much Work is done.
Conclusion: the less you know, the more you make.

Thoreau might have instead reordered the conclusion: the more you make, the less you know.

PUBLIC RELATIONS

No face which we can give to a matter will stead us so well at last as the truth. This alone wears well.

As an accredited public relations professional, I believe this should be the profession's motto.

REAL LONG-TERM ISSUES

While yet it is cold January, and snow and ice are thick and solid, the prudent land-lord comes from the village to get ice to cool his summer drink; impressively, even pathetically, wise, to foresee the heat and thirst of July now in January—wearing a thick coat and mittens! when so many things are not provided for. It may be that he lays up no treasures in this world which will cool his summer drink in the next.

It is incredible how short-term our foresight can be. In the dead of winter I cannot imagine the bare, brown trees covered with a blanket of lush green in the motionless, moist, hot air of a Virginia summer afternoon. It seems with every turn of the seasons, I am surprised again at the new weather patterns, the new colors, the new landscape that unfolds around me. "Geez, can you believe how hot and humid it is?" I say idiotically to people, as if I'd never experienced a Richmond summer, autumn, winter or spring before.

We tend to think that the way it is is the way it will always be, whether we are contemplating the weather or life itself. Financial advisors report that clients planning their estates consistently refer to their impending doom in terms of hopeful uncertainty—e.g., "if I die," rather than "when I die."

Similarly, in business we have created a culture that focuses on the results of the next quarter, rather than the real long-term issues, like a healthy bottom line year-over-year, or employees who do not burn out in a year or two of hard labor, or building a business that can be sustained over the long haul. We can only see the goal right in front of us, and cannot bring ourselves to contemplate the organization that our short-term planning and execution is creating over the long-term.

Thoreau calls us on this. Forget whether you are preparing well enough for what is to come two seasons from now. He asks the harder question—in business or life—are you preparing for the long-term?

REFORM

Statesmen and legislators, standing so completely within the institution, never distinctly and nakedly behold it. They speak of moving society, but have no resting-place without it. (CD)

During my time working for a number of organizations, I've heard a lot of names that the rank and file have had for headquarters and by inference for the executive offices: The Mother Ship, The Palace, The Ivory Tower, Taj Mahal…

Part of the joke is that the leaders back at corporate don't always understand how things really work out in the company, and there is truth to that. It is nearly impossible for the leaders of an organization to get an accurate view that organization from their desks on executive row. So it is no wonder that so many of their decisions, reached via limited and incomplete perspectives, often receive such a poor reception from the worker bees. The warning here is that a leader must be able to step outside her own skewed perspective of an organization and her stake in the status quo if she truly wants to effect meaningful reform.

STATUS ITEMS

When I consider how our houses are built and paid for, or not paid for, and their internal economy managed and sustained, I wonder that the floor does not give way under the visitor while he is admiring the gewgaws upon the mantelpiece, and let him through into the cellar, to some solid and honest though earthy foundation...The first question which I am tempted to put to the proprietor of such great impropriety is, Who bolsters you? Are you one of the ninety-seven who fail, or the three who succeed? Answer me these questions, and then perhaps I may look at your bawbles and find them ornamental. The cart before the horse is neither beautiful nor useful. Before we can adorn our houses with beautiful objects the walls must be stripped, and our lives must be stripped, and beautiful housekeeping and beautiful living be laid for a foundation...

Window dressing merely decorates that which is easily visible from outside, whether in one's home, in one's business or in one's life.

TRADITION AND CULTURE

Commonly men will only be brave as their fathers were brave, or timid. This generation is very sure to plant corn and beans each new year precisely as the Indians did centuries ago and taught the first settlers to do, as if there were a fate in it.

A new husband was cooking a holiday roast for his bride and his own family. With his wife and his mother and grandmother looking on, the husband took out the roast, then (to his wife's horror) cut an inch of meat off each end before putting it in the pan. "Why did you do that?" the wife managed to ask.

"You always cut the ends of the roast off before putting it in the pan," her husband replied confidently. "That's how my mother did it."

"Yes, you always cut off the ends of a roast first," his mother agreed. "That's how my mother did it." The wife then looked to her new grandmother-in-law.

"Well," said grandmother. "When we started out, we didn't have money or nice things, and the only oven pan we could afford was very small. So we had to cut some of the meat off both ends, or it wouldn't fit!"

TRUE UNDERSTANDING

If we knew all the laws of Nature, we should need only one fact, or the description of one actual phenomenon, to infer all the particular results at that point. Now we know only a few laws, and our result is vitiated, not, of course, by any confusion or irregularity in Nature, but by our ignorance of essential elements in the calculation. Our notions of law and harmony are commonly confined to those instances which we detect; but the harmony which results from a far greater number of seemingly conflicting, but really concurring, laws, which we have not detected, is still more wonderful.

True understanding also requires knowing the volume of information that you don't know. We should not be so arrogant as to think that something exists only if we perceive it, or to draw conclusions from only the most easily accessible evidence. Even the most fact-based decisions are made on partial information.

Managing Your People

FLATTERY GETS THEM NOWHERE

I do not wish to flatter my townsmen, nor to be flattered by them, for that will not advance either of us. We need to be provoked—goaded like oxen, as we are, into a trot.

Empty praise and flattery is a de-motivator, both for the employee in question and for the rest of the team looking on. But it is possible to provoke and goad in a positive way: appealing to professional pride; creating challenges; providing the promise of rewards and recognition; and, generally expecting, and seeing, the best in your employees.

HUMAN NEEDS AND MANAGEMENT

The necessaries of life for man in this climate may, accurately enough, be distributed under the several heads of Food, Shelter, Clothing, and Fuel; for not till we have secured these are we prepared to entertain the true problems of life with freedom and a prospect of success.

Thoreau's statement foreshadows Abraham Maslow's Hierarchy Theory, which states that people must meet a set of elemental, basic needs before they can focus on more intangible, higher-level aspirations. Before your company's employees can embrace and achieve the Vision statement that your Vision Committee spent thousands of hours writing and thousands of dollars framing and hanging on the walls, they must have found a way to meet a set of more fundamental needs.

- <u>Physiological</u>: rest, food, drink, shelter, etc. Are your employees working 70 hours a week? Skipping vacations? Missing sleep?

- <u>Safety</u>: not just physical safety, but also consistency, fairness, and a sense of stability and security. These days employee safety is fashionably (and correctly) a critically important issue. Also important are whether employees' work environments are fair and consistent, with stable processes rather than constant chaos, and reasonable security.

- <u>Love and Belonging</u>: loving relationships, a sense of belonging and caring. That <u>doesn't</u> mean co-workers should be "family." It means employees must be allowed to be a part of their <u>own</u> families.

- <u>Esteem</u> (in two ways):

  - Self-respect: confidence, competence, achievement, mastery. These cannot be awarded to an employee, nor can they be achieved by an employee handcuffed by an over-controlling supervisor.

  - Respect from others: acceptance, recognition, appreciation, status. Signs of respect are apparent both in the everyday treatment of employees by their coworkers and supervisors, and the way in which the supervisor and the organization reward good work.

- <u>Understanding and Knowledge</u>: satisfy curiosity, explore, discover solutions, look for meaning, and seek intellectual challenges. Consent to employ innovative thinking must be heart-and-soul a *modus operandi* of your organization every minute of every day. Note that <u>saying</u> (at an off-site, for example) that you support this type of problem-solving approach without actually <u>supporting</u> this type of approach doesn't produce a neutral effect—it seeks out and kills creative thinking like an assassin.

- <u>Aesthetics</u>: *Now* let's talk about landscaping or holiday decorations. Nothing rings in a hollow holiday feeling for defeated employees like empty gift-wrapped boxes under a $10,000 imported tree in the lobby.

- <u>Self-actualization</u>: growth, development and utilization of potential, self-fulfillment. Now you can whip out the Vision statement. Only once employees are allowed the opportunity to meet fundamental needs can they focus on the high ideals contained in this now worthwhile manifesto.

INNOVATORS

Unjust laws exist: shall we be content to obey them, or shall we endeavor to amend them, and obey them until we have succeeded, or shall we transgress them at once? Men, generally, under such a government as this, think that they ought to wait until they have persuaded the majority to alter them. They think that, if they should resist, the remedy would be worse than the evil. But it is the fault of the government itself that the remedy is worse than the evil. It makes it worse. Why is it not more apt to anticipate and provide for reform? Why does it not cherish its wise minority? Why does it cry and resist before it is hurt? Why does it not encourage its citizens to put out its faults, and do better than it would have them? Why does it always crucify Christ and excommunicate Copernicus and Luther, and pronounce Washington and Franklin rebels? (CD)

In his seminal work, *Structures of Scientific Revolutions*, Thomas Kuhn convincingly answers Thoreau's questions. Kuhn showed that people and their organizations are naturally inclined to aggressively resist and attack improvement and innovators. Even innovative organizations have a "way it is done here," as those who challenge the ruling paradigm are sometimes rudely informed. If you're taking fire from all directions, maybe you are challenging sacred—and possibly incorrect—assumptions. And if an employee no longer offers the creative solutions she once did, it may be the culture you have created has beaten the innovative spirit out of her.

LEAD BY EXAMPLE

You who govern public affairs, what need have you to employ punishments? Love virtue, and the people will be virtuous. The virtues of a superior man are like the wind; the virtues of a common man are like the grass—the grass, when the wind passes over it, bends.

A key to personal happiness in life is to align your behavior with your expectations for your own behavior. If you see yourself as someone who values work-life balance, but in reality spend too much time working and not enough time living, the conflict generates cognitive dissonance—the uneasy and unhappy feeling that something is not quite right. Inevitably you modify your behaviors or your expectations to achieve alignment between the two—hopefully you choose to leave unchanged that which is more noble.

Organizations demonstrate a similar dynamic. Senior leadership—and particularly the CEO—sets the expectations of behavior for the organization, sometimes by their words, but most often and effectively by their actions. These expectations sweep over the employees like wind over grass, bending the employee behaviors in its direction.

When the behavior of the employees of an organization does not match the expectations communicated by the leadership, then either the behavior or the expectations will be compelled to change over time. As Thoreau says, usually the employees bend to the example set by senior leadership, and that is where the blame for chronic employee misbehavior should be placed. If that sounds like too much responsibility loaded onto too few shoulders, then don't take the job.

LEADERSHIP AND COMPANY PURPOSE

As for the Pyramids, there is nothing to wonder at in them so much as the fact that so many men could be found degraded enough to spend their lives constructing a tomb for some ambitious booby, whom it would have been wiser and manlier to have drowned in the Nile, and then given his body to the dogs.

Are you working for a CEO or a Pharaoh? Or, even scarier, if you're the boss…which of these do your employees think you are? It's even worse than figuring out that you're the pointy-haired boss from Dilbert.

LEARNING

Which would have advanced the most at the end of a month—the boy who had made his own jackknife from the ore which he had dug and smelted, reading as much as would be necessary for this—or the boy who had attended the lectures on metallurgy at the Institute in the meanwhile, and had received a Rodgers' penknife from his father? Which would be most likely to cut his fingers?

Consider the process of learning how to use a computer. When do you learn more: while reading the manual with the computer in the box, or while attempting (and often failing) to actually use the damn thing? Real-life experience, whether as part of a structured schooling process or "audited" by the willing student outside a formal program, is the best teacher.

LOYALTY

Yet some can be patriotic who have no self-respect, and sacrifice the greater to the less. They love the soil which makes their graves, but have no sympathy with the spirit which may still animate their clay.

Blind patriotism can infect a company as easily as a country. Managers who exercise and demand a "my company right or wrong"-brand of patriotism succeed mainly in killing or driving out the spirit that leads to creative thinking and innovative solutions. Even worse, loyalty to company rather than to ideals is the sort of belief system that can result in the commission and/or cover-up of illegal or unsafe activities.

MATURING

It is not important that he should mature as soon as an apple tree or an oak. Shall he turn his spring into summer? If the condition of things which we were made for is not yet, what were any reality which we can substitute? We will not be shipwrecked on a vain reality.

To use another analogy, it is OK to have your receiver rehearse pass patterns during practice, but don't forget that this is only practice. The yardage won't count until the quarterback throws the live pass during the game, so there's not much use in having the defensive back take the receiver's head off during the scrimmage.

Give young or new employees work that helps them practice, but don't rush them to be ready and punish them for their mistakes before the tasks that they are training for even exist.

NATURE OF TRUTH

The particular laws are as our points of view, as, to the traveller, a mountain outline varies with every step, and it has an infinite number of profiles, though absolutely but one form. Even when cleft or bored through it is not comprehended in its entireness.

A great thing about being the boss getting to define what is "true"—what "reality" the organization puts its resources against. But the smart boss knows that hers is only one version of the "truth," and that there are as many sides as there are people considering it.

For example, I thought I knew what the Rock of Gibraltar looked like. But I learned, sailing around it at the end of a transatlantic journey, that the famous outcrop shows its most familiar profile from only one angle. From any other perspective, it took on very unfamiliar shapes. From this I learned that "the truth" can vary depending on your perspective; that is, from where you are viewing the issue. And while there may be "truth" to the most popularly held version, or the version that is enforceable by organizational structure, it is foolish to assume that it is the only truth that exists.

PERSUASION

Thaw with his gentle persuasion is more powerful than Thor with his hammer. The one melts, the other but breaks in pieces.

As it relates to managing people, when you read this quote think of the ice as the employee's heart and soul. In our incredibly fast-paced, high-pressure business environment, sometimes the hammer is the most convenient tool to pull out. But I've seen too many times that a single ill-advised application of that tool can leave an employee unwilling to take a risk or to innovate, leaving the employee, the team and the manager poorer off as a result.

PERSPECTIVE

Why should we be in such desperate haste to succeed and in such desperate enterprises? If a man does not keep pace with his companions, perhaps it is because he hears a different drummer. Let him step to the music which he hears, however measured or far away.

It is easy to fall into the value system that is so prevalent in today's workplace, where our estimated worth often is a reflection of titles, office size, hours behind the desk and number of direct reports. A coworker who marches to the beat of a different drummer will appear out of step with this twisted ethic. If you manage such a person, treasure that—the rugged individualism that enables this employee to hear and march to her own music also can be a source of rare, innovative, break-out thinking.

QUESTIONING THE RULES

It is said that Mirabeau took to highway robbery "to ascertain what degree of resolution was necessary in order to place one's self in formal opposition to the most sacred laws of society."... This was manly, as the world goes; and yet it was idle, if not desperate. A saner man would have found himself often enough "in formal opposition" to what are deemed "the most sacred laws of society," through obedience to yet more sacred laws, and so have tested his resolution without going out of his way.

The "troublemakers" in your organization who seem to question every rule may be answering to a higher ideal—even a higher authority. Maybe there is some room for improvement in our policy manual after all. Let's check...hmm..., under Section III, Subsection G, Paragraph 5...

SOURCES OF WISDOM

Early in the morning, while all things are crisp with frost, men come with fishing-reels and slender lunch, and let down their fine lines through the snowy field to take pickerel and perch; wild men, who instinctively follow other fashions and trust other authorities than their townsmen, and by their goings and comings stitch towns together in parts where else they would be ripped. They sit and eat their luncheon in stout fear-naughts on the dry oak leaves on the shore, as wise in natural lore as the citizen is in artificial. They never consulted with books, and know and can tell much less than they have done. The things which they practice are said not yet to be known....His life itself passes deeper in nature than the studies of the naturalist penetrate; himself a subject for the naturalist. The latter raises the moss and bark gently with his knife in search of insects; the former lays open logs to their core with his axe, and moss and bark fly far and wide.

There is studying life and there is living life, and there is a lot to learn from the latter that you will not learn from the former. All wisdom does not reside with the polished MBAs.

Managing Your Working Relationships
(boss, coworkers, associates, vendors)

CUBICLE LIVING

...we live thick and are in each other's way, and stumble over one another, and I think that we thus lose some respect for one another.

These days, when only those who should be leading by example have offices, and the rest of us are spread like crop seed out in cubicle farms, even the friendliest coworkers can get on each other's nerves.

Considerate behavior can still leave room enough to stumble over one another in our daily work, and sometimes the collaborative design of our office space leads us to collaboratively drive each other nuts.

During these tense moments, it is a good idea to follow Thoreau's example and get away from it all. That doesn't mean you go live in the woods for a couple years. A lunch away from your desk, a walk through the office park, a quiet corner in the library, stolen minutes in a coffee shop—there are many ways get out of the thick, out of each other's way, and preserve that respect for the other.

CYNICISM

Some would find fault with the morning red, if they ever got up early enough.

I have been in work environments that were so bad, even the most bitter cynics fell short of the mark in their complaints. But more often I have experienced good and even excellent work environments. Yet, the cynics never go away. Even in the best situations, it seems some people cannot move beyond complaining, blaming, gossiping and backstabbing.

Don't let these chronic complainers dim the beauty that you see in life, in your company, in your day-to-day work experience. You do not need to condemn them or avoid them if you can separate your beliefs and perceptions from theirs—after all, these might be your coworkers, friends or even your manager. Keep in mind though that in most conversations, a cynic will set the tone, and it can be very difficult to pull a person or group of people to your level of existence when they are mired in the tar pit of cynicism.

But no matter what, don't let them drag you in with them.

EVOLUTION

For the improvements of ages have had but little influence on the essential laws of man's existence; as our skeletons, probably, are not to be distinguished from those of our ancestors.

The common, immutable laws of decency and humanity will always apply, regardless of whether you interact with others in person, over the phone, by fax, on the Internet or by wireless device.

GENIUS

Sometimes we are inclined to class those who are once-and-a-half-witted with the half-witted, because we appreciate only a third part of their wit.

My friend, Dr. Darryl Pearlman (also my dentist, so I try to stay on his good side) and I have held a version of this theory (mostly out of comic arrogance, I'm sure) for years when it comes to our humor: if they're not laughing, it may not be because it's not funny, but because they don't get it.

But seriously folks, when extended to business, this quote from Thoreau should give reassurance to all those whose ideas and contributions are not appreciated, or worse, are ignored. Take heart. There is a good chance that the audience does not appreciate 2/3 of your genius.

GENUINE FELLOWSHIP

Rather than love, than money, than fame, give me truth. I sat at a table where were rich food and wine in abundance, and obsequious attendance, but sincerity and truth were not; and I went away hungry from the inhospitable board.

For two years during my late twenties, I was a staffer on Capitol Hill. The experience was a rush—interacting daily with nationally known legislators, news personalities, political operatives and the smartest, most ambitious young people I'd ever met.

Often we would work late on some important issue or media event, then all go out to one of the local establishments for dinner. The conversation was sharp and witty, the spirits flowed freely, and the atmosphere was as intoxicating as the drink.

Yet, but for precious exceptions, I never felt really secure in many of these relationships, and often I felt compelled to leave the table in the middle of the festivities, find a pay phone in some secluded and semi-quiet section of the bar, and call my brother or one of my two sisters—just to talk to someone with whom I knew for certain exactly where I stood.

HUMILITY

Humility like darkness reveals the heavenly lights.

Sometimes the light we try to shed on our accomplishments by calling attention to them actually has the effect of diminishing the relative brightness of those accomplishments. There are times when you should talk about what you've done, and there are other times when it is wisest to let those achievements speak for themselves.

MISERY LOVES COMPANY

But, wherever a man goes, men will pursue and paw him with their dirty institutions, and, if they can, constrain him to belong to their desperate odd-fellow society.

Cynicism in the workplace may be the most insidious of these dirty institutions. Cynicism occurs when the urge to improve a situation is hijacked by pessimism and negativity. How you move through life and work is your choice. Stay positive, stay constructive…don't let others pull you into misery with them.

PASSIVE HEROISM

It is not a man's duty, as a matter of course, to devote himself to the eradication of any, even to the most enormous, wrong; he may still properly have other concerns to engage him; but it is his duty, at least, to wash his hands of it, and, if he gives it no thought longer, not to give it practically his support. (CD)

"The only thing necessary for the triumph of evil is for good men to do nothing." So reportedly said Edmund Burke, Irish philosopher and statesman—an impossible challenge if applied to every evil encountered at work.

Heck, I've seen people pull more dirty tricks before the 9 a.m. staff meeting than Machiavelli could have gotten to all day. Dedicate yourself to righting every wrong in Corporate America and you won't last much past lunch. Put another way: there's only one well-executed suicide mission in any of us.

Thoreau gives us another option: don't enable evil. Steer clear of rumors, backstabbing and vilification of others. Over time, even small constructive actions at work lace the workplace with a positive antidote to poisonous practices, and improve the atmosphere.

POSITIVE INTENT

This further experience also I gained: I said to myself, I will not plant beans and corn with so much industry another summer, but such seeds, if the seed is not lost, as sincerity, truth, simplicity, faith, innocence, and the like, and see if they will not grow in this soil...and sustain me...

Amid mergers and downsizing, coworkers often seem more like rivals than teammates, and the "sincerity, truth, simplicity, faith, innocence, and the like" seem idealistic. Instead we expect treachery and sabotage, exploitation of our mistakes and the stealing of our successes. Even family photos on coworkers' desks seem placed with Machiavellian calculation.

But what if...we viewed coworkers as humans, like us: fathers or mothers, sons or daughters, the love of someone's life. In this light, they no longer are enemies with malicious agendas, but instead are teammates who may disagree with our opinions, but primarily are doing the best they know how for the company. With which would you be more cooperative?

It may feel like unilateral disarmament—but to sow and grow the higher human qualities in yourself, you need to view those who hold opposing opinions as fellow good souls acting out of positive intent and trying to survive in the harsh environment of 21st Century Corporate America.

SELF-ESTEEM

Public opinion is a weak tyrant compared with our own private opinion. What a man thinks of himself, that it is which determines, or rather indicates, his fate.

Have you ever noticed that everyone at work has a theory on everyone else in the office? Bring up any coworker at lunch, and everyone at the table will tell you authoritatively what motivates that person and what his agenda is.

What cracks me up is the idea that, if everyone at lunch has a theory on everyone else in the office, they probably have a theory about me too. Which tells me they also have way too much time on their hands.

All jokes aside, your opinion of yourself is critical, because you always will move in the direction of your thoughts. If you buy into others' opinions of you, you will subconsciously move in that direction, fulfilling the prophesy that someone else has for you. If you buy into your own opinion of yourself (positive or negative), you will move in that self-selected direction, regardless of what others think of you.

SOCIAL INTERACTION

Every day or two I strolled to the village to hear some of the gossip which is incessantly going on there, circulating either from mouth to mouth, or from newspaper to newspaper, and which, taken in homoeopathic doses, was really as refreshing in its way as the rustle of leaves and the peeping of frogs.

It is possible to sample the trivial without being driven by it. In fact, it is often only through bitch sessions or lunches with a side dish of grapevine that you can meet some coworkers or employees. You don't have to spread rumors to hear them, and it is important that you know what is on the minds of your coworkers and employees.

TRUTH

The volatile truth of our words should continually betray the inadequacy of the residual statement. Their truth is instantly translated; its literal monument alone remains.

In his classic political and human relations primmer *Hardball*, Chris Matthews quotes Senator Edmond S. Muskie of Maine as saying "Only talk when it improves the silence." This is Thoreau's corollary to that warning, for use in instances where there is not silence but instead foolish chatter.

TRUTH (II)

Say what you have to say, not what you ought. Any truth is better than make-believe.

You do not provide value to your boss or your organization when you state anything other than what you believe about a situation. That's not to say, of course, that you need to bludgeon people with your view of the truth. "Say what you have to say, not what you ought," yes, but you should say what you have to say in the way you ought to say it.

Peggy Noonan, in her book about her years as a speechwriter in the White House, *What I Saw at the Revolution*, put this another way when she relayed advice her boss once gave her: "You can call a spade a spade, but you don't have to call it a sh*t-shovel."

VALUE OF A DOLLAR

Money is not required to buy one necessary of the soul.

Money is not required to buy one necessary of another's soul either. The souls of good employees are not acquired only with money.

Managing The Business
Environment
(Society, Government,
Culture, etc.)

CORPORATE WELFARE

Most think that they are above being supported by the town; but it oftener happens that they are not above supporting themselves by dishonest means, which should be more disreputable.

Incentives such tax credits or new roads to build a plant in a particular area are examples of the government looking after the businesses' welfare. It makes sense, because it is in the interests of the government and its citizens to help the business to thrive. For that matter, mortgage interest tax credits for individuals are the government's way of looking after tax-paying citizens' welfare.

Now, I was an early adopter of the idea that citizens on welfare should work whenever possible for their benefits—I remember my patronizing girlfriend back in 1987 saying that expecting these folks to work was "a little unrealistic, don't you think?" But I think we in the middle and upper classes could be a little more honest with ourselves when we criticize the idea of welfare for poor people, given our glass homes and glass factories that have been paid for, in part, through government assistance.

DEMAND BETTER

But, to speak practically and as a citizen, unlike those who call themselves no-govern-ment men, I ask for, not at once no government, but at once a better government. Let every man make known what kind of government would command his respect, and that will be one step toward obtaining it. (CD)

It's been said we get the government we deserve. When only 50% of eligible voters take part in the political process, we get the same result as when 50% of the parents in a household take part in raising the child.

But this quote isn't just about government, or about family. It is about our communities and our places of work. Yes, the CEO ultimately is accountable for culture and climate in the workplace, but it is an accountability for which he or she has only limited capability to control. Recalling Longfellow's words that, in this world, man is either hammer or anvil: If you choose hammer, then the anvil upon which you shape your world will be your government, your community and your company. Choose anvil, and your government, community and com-pany will be the hammers that shape your world. Choose hammer.

FREE ENTERPRISE

Governments show thus how successfully men can be imposed upon, even impose on themselves, for their own advantage. It is excellent, we must all allow. Yet this government never of itself furthered any enterprise, but by the alacrity with which it got out of its way. It does not keep the country free. It does not settle the West. It does not educate. The character inherent in the American people has done all that has been accomplished; and it would have done somewhat more, if the government had not sometimes got in its way. (CD)

Not even during the Revolutionary period would this statement have been as revolutionary as it seems today.

LEGALLY RIGHT V. MORALLY RIGHT

I think that we should be men first, and subjects afterward. It is not desirable to culti-vate a respect for the law, so much as for the right. The only obligation which I have a right to assume is to do at any time what I think right. (CD)

No offense to my hard-core Democrat friends out there, but Bill Clinton proved that you can be a (mostly) law-abiding citizen and a scoundrel simulta-neously. Laws are a standard of desperation, by which we protect ourselves from ourselves, rather than a standard of aspiration, by which we would improve our-selves and our communities. In this light, the term "law-abiding citizen" is one of the worst backhanded compliments possible. Someone who has merely obeyed the law throughout his life has done the absolute minimum necessary to get by.

Now apply that to business. It is possible for a company to act within laws, regulations and reporting rules and still be dishonest in its actions and in its cul-ture. When executives talk to employees, investors, communities or the govern-ment, they should be guided not by what is legally required, but by what is morally right.

PROGRESS

Men think that it is essential that the Nation have commerce, and export ice, and talk through a telegraph, and ride thirty miles an hour, without a doubt, whether they do or not; but whether we should live like baboons or like men, is a little uncertain. If we do not get out sleepers, and forge rails, and devote days and nights to the work, but go to tinkering upon our lives to improve them, who will build railroads? And if railroads are not built, how shall we get to heaven in season? But if we stay at home and mind our business, who will want railroads?

Progress of any kind, like a railroad, is only useful if we know where we want it to take us, and why.

REGULATION

Trade and commerce, if they were not made of india-rubber, would never manage to bounce over obstacles which legislators are continually putting in their way; and if one were to judge these men wholly by the effects of their actions and not partly by their intentions, they would deserve to be classed and punished with those mischievous persons who put obstructions on the railroads. (CD)

Controls and governance (which are both imposed from without by the government and imposed from within by the company) are critically important in any business—ask anyone who held stock in Enron. The most effective controls and governance, though, are those regulations that encourage, guide or restrict actions while leaving the fewest fingerprints.

TWO SIDES TO THE CORPORATE STORY

These beans have results which are not harvested by me. Do they not grow for wood-chucks partly? The ear of wheat (in Latin spica, obsoletely speca, from spe, hope) should not be the only hope of the husbandman; its kernel or grain (granum from ger-endo, bearing) is not all that it bears. How, then, can our harvest fail? Shall I not rejoice also at the abundance of the weeds whose seeds are the granary of the birds? It matters little comparatively whether the fields fill the farmer's barns.

We hear a lot about the evils of corporations, from scandalously high CEO pay and obscenely low employee pay to a myriad concerns about companies' negative effects on our community, nation and world. No doubt some charges have merit, but the complainers don't often acknowledge the positive effects. Beyond the direct benefit of employment, there are indirect benefits, for vendors, local restaurants, product wholesalers and retailers, government (through company taxes), charitable organizations—even, if they thought about it, for the complainers themselves. Obviously, the negative aspects of corporate America need addressing. But there are two sides to this story, even if you regularly hear about only one of them.

VIRTUE OF CAPITALISM

What recommends commerce to me is its enterprise and bravery. It does not clasp its hands and pray to Jupiter.

Like God, capitalism helps those who help themselves.

VIRTUE OF CAPITALISM (II)

Commerce is unexpectedly confident and serene, alert, adventurous, and unwearied. It is very natural in its methods withal, far more so than many fantastic enterprises and sentimental experiments, and hence its singular success.

Commerce is the natural extension of the instinctive human drive to move forward. It is what it is and doesn't pretend to be otherwise.

Conclusion

In the end, what Thoreau offers is freedom. Freedom from false values. Freedom from imposed expectations. Freedom to find who we really are, and then to live as that person. Freedom to dream of a better life, and then to live that dream.

If one "endeavors to live the life which he has imagined," Thoreau offers freedom from the life-limiting, soul-killing conventions of our culture. These conventions are derived from a collective lack of courage, and manifested through conventional wisdom, peer pressure, parochialism, the twin assassins of "we don't do it that way" and "not invented here," and a societal phobia of failure.

All of it conspires to convince us that we are naive to want to live differently, fools to aspire to a better way. "There *is* no other way," we are told (by the well-intentioned and otherwise). But Thoreau challenges that conclusion, and challenges us: "*Why do you stay here and live this mean moiling life, when a glorious existence is possible for you?*"

The time has come for you to take up that challenge, and to create your glorious existence. Thoreau shows the way, and brings the good news that the universe is ready to help us, once we begin:

"*...if one advances confidently in the direction of his dreams, and endeavors to live the life which he has imagined, he will meet with a success unexpected in common hours. He will put some things behind, will pass an invisible boundary; new, universal, and more liberal laws will begin to establish themselves around and within him; or the old laws be expanded, and interpreted in his favor in a more liberal sense, and he will live with the license of a higher order of beings.*"

Do not shy away from what seems to be the impossible, because what we think is impossible is only so if we continue to live by the constraints that our society and our fellow man have placed upon us.

Aspire to an existence worthy of your imagination, and then bring your reality into alignment with that. Build your castles in the air. Thoreau is right: that is where they should be. Commit your plan to paper, map out the steps you'll need to take and the things you'll need to learn and the help you'll need to seek out. And then take action, every day, to put foundations under your castles built in the air.

Acknowledgments

This book would never have become a reality without the loving support of my wife Stacy. She has been a constant source of encouragement and confidence as I've worked on this and other writing projects—even when the honey-do list was running long and severely neglected.

I also thank our children, Daniel and Madison, who provide us with a daily, living, laughing, loving reminder of what really is important in this life, how lucky we are, and how we are obligated to live this gift of life to the fullest, every day.

I am grateful for the support of my family: Mom, Dad, my sister Kathy and her husband Doug, my brother Ken and his wife KT, and my sister Linda and her husband Lee. I especially want to thank Lee, who may in fact be the reincarnation of Henry David Thoreau, for reintroducing me to *Walden* at a time in my life when I was searching, not only for answers, but for a better way to find answers. And I want to thank Stacy's family, who at no point over the ten years I've been working to build my writing career ever expressed a doubt that I would be successful.

Special thanks go out to Elsbeth Wetherill—an exceptional advisor, supporter and friend. Thank you for working so hard to make this book a reality.

No success is ever achieved without the help of others. I have been lucky to have writing and publishing mentors—Joan Tupponce, Charlie Slack, Will Schwalbe and Larry Kamerman—who took time from their busy and successful careers to pass along wisdom and much-needed encouragement. Thank you, each of you.

I also want to thank my friend, Chip Noonan, who saw the book that this should be when I was still looking at it as a manuscript, and prodded me to live what I'd written.

Over the years I have accumulated vast riches in the form of friends and supporters who have enthusiastically welcomed my little bulletins regarding my progress, or lack thereof, in becoming a "real" writer. Thank you for your encouragement. By treating me like a success from the beginning, you helped prove once again the principle of self-fulfilling prophesies.

Build Your Castles in the Air is the fortunate beneficiary of positive endorsements from several of the people I admire most in the world. I want to extend my deep-felt gratitude to all of those who offered advance praise for this book: Louis Castle, Diane Shanklin, Craig Shanklin, Victoria Guthrie, Congresswoman Susan Molinari, and Dr. Wayne Dyer.

I am honored beyond words to have Nigel Morris as the author of the foreword for this book. I do not think it is an overstatement to say that there are few men or women who have accomplished so much, who have enabled and empowered so many to achieve self-actualization, as Nigel Morris did by helping to found and grow the Fortune 200 company Capital One over just a few short years. A few more like him in this world might actually change this world. He certainly helped change mine.

And finally, as Daniel, Madison and Stacy and I say every night, I want to thank God for this beautiful day, for each other and the chance He's given us to be together, for His son Jesus, and for the gift of life.

About the Author

Before finding his direction in life, Chuck drifted through many jobs, including copier salesman, stand-up comic, blackjack dealer, telemarketer, substitute teacher, private detective and donut maker. At 25, Chuck drifted to St. Thomas on a one-way plane ticket, where he came of age through a series of adventures, starting as a bouncer in a rough-and-tumble working-sailors' bar and ending up as crew on a 53-foot sloop sailing across the North Atlantic.

Chuck stepped off that boat in Ibiza in the Mediterranean Sea a changed man, at the helm of his life and charting a new course. He earned a masters degree in communications and professional accreditation, served as press secretary for a member of Congress, speechwriter for a Virginia governor, communications director for a Virginia secretary of transportation, director of Virginia's Adopt-a-Highway program, and as an executive speechwriter with three Fortune 500 companies. Chuck currently is a writer with Capital One Financial Corp.

Chuck is a motivational speaker, pens a monthly humor column for *Home Style* magazine and a quarterly column for *WorkMagazine*, and his humor appears frequently other publications such as *Richmond Magazine*, *Richmond Bride* magazine and *Welcome Inc.* magazine.

Chuck and Stacy Hansen have two children, Daniel (9) and Madison (7), and live in Midlothian, Virginia.

CHUCK'S WRITING

Chuck Hansen's writing regularly appears in magazines and on Web sites, and he has several other book projects underway, including *Crossing a Big Ocean*, an account of his astonishing experiences living in the Caribbean and crossing the North Atlantic on a 53-foot sailboat. To engage Chuck to write an article for your publication, get the latest information on his writing projects, find links to current and past magazine articles or request clips, or subscribe to Chuck's e-newsletter, email him at chuck@chuckhansen.com or visit www.chuck-hansen.com.

MOTIVATIONAL SPEAKING

Chuck Hansen can be a speaker at your next meeting or event, presenting his perspective on the power of Henry David Thoreau's words in our modern world. Participants in these sessions will get:

- Immediate strategies for handling the chaos of the typical business day, with working materials that the participants keep

- A foundational approach for life focusing on the big picture and the truly important, rather than on artificial emergencies, and based on the timeless wisdom of Henry David Thoreau

- From this balance springs the opportunity for increased productivity, both professionally and personally

- Insight for gaining true personal freedom

The presentation is based on *Build Your Castles in the Air: Thoreau's Inspiring Advice for Success in Business (and Life) in the 21st Century*. This book can be made available to each participant as part of the speaking engagement.

For details on this and other presentation topics, availability, references and more, contact Chuck at chuck@chuckhansen.com or at www.chuckhansen.com.

978-0-595-37251-5
0-595-37251-1